The Primary Source Library of Famous Explorers™

Amerigo Vespucci
A Primary Source Biography

Lynn Hoogenboom

The Rosen Publishing Group's
PowerKids Press™
PRIMARY SOURCE

New York

For Meredith

Published in 2006 by The Rosen Publishing Group, Inc.
29 East 21st Street, New York, NY 10010

First Edition

Editor: Daryl Heller
Book Design: Albert B. Hanner
Layout Design: Greg Tucker
Photo Researcher: Jeffrey Wendt

Photo Credits: Cover, p. 14 (top) National Library of Australia, Canberra, Australia / Bridgeman Art Library; pp. 5 (left), 18 Bildarchiv Preussischer Kulturbesitz / Art Resource, NY; p. 5 (right) map by Greg Tucker; p. 6 (left) Palazzo Medici-Riccardi, Florence, Italy / Bridgeman Art Library; p. 6 (right) Alinari / Art Resource, NY; p. 9 (top) Monastery of La Rabida, Huelva, Andalusia, Spain / Bridgeman Art Library; p. 9 (bottom) © The Board of Trustees of the Armouries; p. 10 Courtesy of the Rare Books Division, The New York Public Library, Astor, Lenox and Tilden Foundations; p. 13 (top) Archives Charmet / Bridgeman Art Library; p. 13 (bottom) Library of Congress Geography and Map Division; p. 14 (bottom) Trachtenbuch, Germanisches National Museum; p. 17 akg-images; p. 21 (top) Scala / Art Resource, NY; p. 21 (bottom) © National Maritime Museum, London, Barberini Collection.

Library of Congress Cataloging-in-Publication Data

Hoogenboom, Lynn.
Amerigo Vespucci : a primary source biography / Lynn Hoogenboom.
p. cm. — (The primary source library of famous explorers) Includes index.
ISBN 1-4042-3037-8 (library binding)
1. Vespucci, Amerigo, 1451–1512—Juvenile literature. 2. Explorers—America—Biography—Juvenile literature. 3. Explorers—Spain—Biography—Juvenile literature. 4. Explorers—Portugal—Biography—Juvenile literature. 5. America—Discovery and exploration—Spanish—Juvenile literature. 6. America—Discovery and exploration—Portuguese—Juvenile literature. 7. South America—Discovery and exploration—Spanish—Juvenile literature. I. Title.

E125.V5H66 2006
970.01'6'092—dc22

2004030234

Manufactured in the United States of America

Contents

Man of Mystery

Amerigo Vespucci may be the most mysterious of all the famous explorers. This is because historians cannot agree on whether he was a great explorer or a fake.

Vespucci was born on March 9, 1454, in Florence, Italy. He was the third of four sons born to Nastagio and Elisabetta Vespucci. His father was a notary. This is a person who checks important papers to make sure they are **legal** and then marks them as official.

Amerigo attended a school that was run by his uncle Giorgio Antonio Vespucci. The sons of many of the most respected families in Florence, including the Vespuccis, went to that school. The boys were taught math, **geography**, Latin, and literature, which is the study of written works such as books and poetry.

Amerigo Vespucci also learned a lot outside of school. At that time some of the world's finest artists, poets, and musicians lived in Florence.

When the explorer Amerigo Vespucci was a boy, there were suddenly major accomplishments in science, music, art, and the written word. This period was called the Renaissance. It began in the 1300s in Italy and was at its height in Florence when Vespucci was growing up.

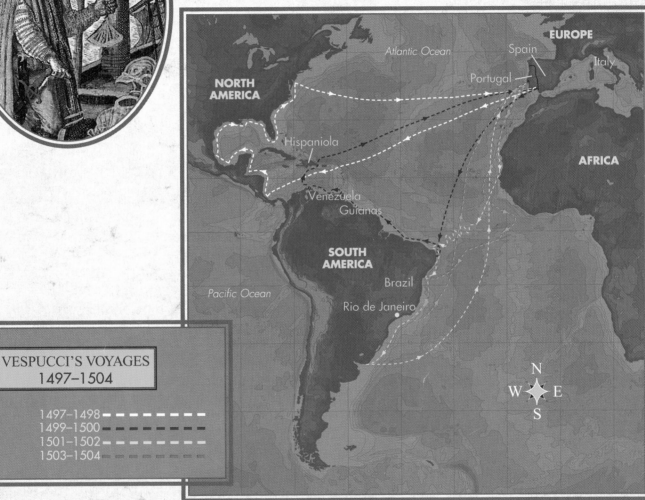

EUROPE
Atlantic Ocean
Spain
Portugal
Italy
NORTH AMERICA
AFRICA
Hispaniola
Venezuela
Guianas
SOUTH AMERICA
Brazil
Pacific Ocean
Rio de Janeiro

N
W E
S

VESPUCCI'S VOYAGES
1497–1504

1497–1498
1499–1500
1501–1502
1503–1504

This map shows the four voyages Amerigo Vespucci made to the New World between 1497 and 1504. Many historians think Vespucci did not actually make the voyage to the New World in 1497 that is shown in white above.

The wealthy banker and Florentine leader Lorenzo de' Medici was a patron of the arts. This means that he gave money to artists to help them create their work. The artists he helped included Leonardo da Vinci and Michelangelo.

This 1700s painting of Florence, Italy, by an unknown artist, was based on an earlier work done around 1480. The original was a detail, or a close-up, of the city, which appeared on a map of Florence.

The pope became angry with Florence in 1478 after the citizens of Florence hanged the Archbishop of Pisa, a church official. The citizens of Florence did so because the archbishop had planned with other men to murder Lorenzo de' Medici's brother, Giuliano. These men tried, unsuccessfully, to kill Lorenzo, too.

Early Jobs

In 1478, Amerigo Vespucci became an **assistant** to a diplomat, Guido Antonio Vespucci, who was his father's cousin. A diplomat represents, or acts for, his or her own government in its dealings with other governments.

Italy was not yet a country, so Guido Antonio represented Florence, which was an independent Italian city. A powerful family of bankers, the Medici, controlled Florence's government. Lorenzo de' Medici, who was known as Lorenzo the Magnificent, was the family's leader.

During this same time, the **pope**, who is the head of the Catholic Church, warned that Florence would be banned from the church. Anyone who did business with Florence would be thrown out of the Catholic Church. As Guido Antonio's assistant, Amerigo traveled to the Italian cities of Bologna and Milan, as well as to France, to gain **support** for Florence. In 1482, Amerigo took a job handling business affairs for a branch of the Medici family headed by another Lorenzo. His name was Lorenzo the Popolano.

Vespucci Helps Columbus

In 1492, Amerigo Vespucci moved to Seville, Spain. That same year King Ferdinand and Queen Isabella of Spain agreed to support the first **voyage** of Christopher Columbus. Columbus thought he could discover a new **trade route** from Europe to Asia by sailing west, rather than around Africa. Ferdinand and Isabella gave Columbus only part of the money required for the voyage. He needed **investors** for the rest. Most investors were Italians living in Spain. One such investor was Gianetto Berardi, a merchant and banker. Vespucci had begun working for him when he arrived in Seville.

Columbus returned to Spain from America in March 1493. Berardi and Vespucci helped Columbus prepare for his second voyage by getting him ships, cannons, and food supplies. After Berardi died in 1495, Vespucci became the head of his business. Vespucci helped Columbus prepare for his third voyage of May 1498. It was on this voyage that Columbus reached the **mainland** of South America.

Columbus left Palos, Spain, in August 1492, with three ships. Gianetto Berardi and Amerigo Vespucci were businessmen who helped Columbus prepare for this voyage to the New World. The two men knew the owners and the captains of the three ships.

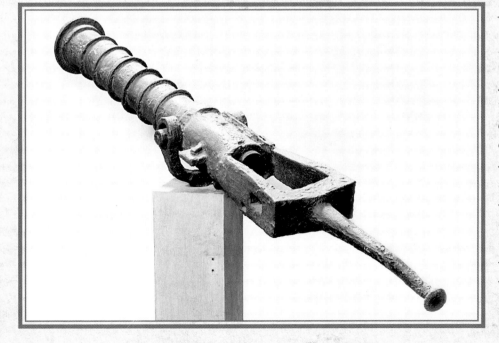

Berardi and Vespucci lent Columbus money to purchase supplies, such as cannons, for his voyage. The European explorers armed themselves with small cannons such as this early 1500s swivel gun when they came to the New World. The gun could swivel, which means that it could be turned from one side to another to fire at a target. A target is something or someone that the shooter wants to harm.

From Amerigo Vespucci's 1504
letter to Piero Soderini

"The chief cause which moved me
to write to you, was at the request
of the present bearer; who is
named Benvenuto Benvenuti ...
[who] begged that I should make
communication to your
Magnificence of the things seen by
me in divers regions of the world,
by virtue of four voyages which I
have made in discovery of new
lands ... We set out from the port
of Cadiz on the 10th day of May
1497, and took our route through
the great gulf of the Ocean-sea: in
which voyage we were eighteen
months engaged and discovered
much continental land and
innumerable islands, and great
part of them inhabited. ..."

At the advice of Benvenuto
Benvenuti, Vespucci wrote to Piero
Soderini, an Italian official, about
his four voyages to the New World.
Vespucci writes that after leaving
Cadiz, Spain, in May 1497, they
crossed the Atlantic Ocean and
spent 18 months exploring the
Americas and their coastal
islands. Many of these areas had
people living there.

This is a copy of a letter that Vespucci wrote to Piero
Soderini in 1504. Soderini was an official in Florence.
This Italian copy of Vespucci's letter was printed in 1885.
In this letter Vespucci talked about four voyages to the
New World, including a voyage taken in 1497.

The Questionable Voyage of 1497

In a letter written in 1504, Amerigo Vespucci wrote that his first voyage to the New World took place in 1497. This was a year before Columbus reached the South American mainland. However, there are records showing that Vespucci was doing business in Spain in 1497. This means that he could not have been sailing along the coast of Mexico in 1497, as he claimed in his letter.

Some historians think Vespucci made up the 1497 voyage. They think Vespucci wanted the **credit** that should have gone to Columbus for being the first person to reach the American mainland. However, neither Vespucci nor Columbus realized that it would be an honor to be the first to reach America. Both explorers believed that the new land was close to Asia, which people already knew about. There was no good reason for Vespucci to lie. Columbus was also a friend of Vespucci's. In 1505, Columbus wrote to his son Diego, "Amerigo Vespucci has always **behaved** properly toward me; he is a very honest man."

Sailing to the New World

Historians are sure that Amerigo Vespucci did sail to America in 1499. On this voyage he was a gentleman volunteer. This was someone who probably helped pay for the **expedition** and was treated like an officer.

Alonso de Ojeda led this expedition, which landed in South America in the area that is the modern-day Guianas. From there they sailed west along the coast of modern-day Venezuela. "The trees are so beautiful and so soft that we thought we were in the **Garden of Eden**," Vespucci later wrote in 1504. In June 1500, after almost a year of exploration, the expedition returned to Seville.

The next time Vespucci sailed, it was for Manuel, king of Portugal. Vespucci was asked by the king to join the Portuguese expedition because he knew a lot about **navigation** and had sailed close to modern-day Brazil when he sailed with Ojeda. King Manuel wanted to explore this area, which belonged to Portugal after the 1494 **Treaty of Tordesillas** was signed.

This painting shows Amerigo Vespucci guiding a ship by celestial navigation. When a ship is in the middle of the ocean, a celestial navigator must judge the placement of the night stars. He or she uses this knowledge to decide where he or she is, and in what direction to sail the ship next. Some historians question Vespucci's skill at celestial navigation.

This 1500s map shows the separation of the land and seas set by the 1494 Treaty of Tordesillas. The line that runs north to south at the center of the map shows the separation of Portuguese and Spanish lands and seas.

On May 5, 1493, Pope Alexander VI divided, or separated, all the undiscovered land in the world between Spain and Portugal. The pope drew an imaginary line in the middle of the Atlantic Ocean. Portugal objected, and in the 1494 Treaty of Tordesillas, Spain agreed to move the line far enough to give Portugal Newfoundland in the North and Brazil in the South.

The beauty of South America captivated Vespucci. As he traveled he took notes on the many different people, flowers, animals, trees, and stars that he saw. Shown here is the Bay of Rio de Janeiro, which Vespucci reached in January 1502. Sugarloaf Mountain is in the background.

The German artist Christopher Weiditz drew this picture of a Native American in 1529. Amerigo Vespucci and the Portuguese sailors who accompanied him on the 1501 trip to Brazil charmed the Native Americans with small gifts, such as beads, bells, and mirrors. Unfortunately, many Native Americans were forced to become slaves to the Europeans, either in the New World colonies or across the Atlantic Ocean in Europe.

The Portuguese Voyages

In May 1501, King Manuel asked Amerigo Vespucci to sail as an **adviser** to Gonzalo Coelho, who was leading an expedition to Brazil. They reached South America on August 17, 1501, then traveled south along the Brazilian coast. They had trouble with some Native American nations, but they sometimes stayed in friendly Indian villages for several days. On January 1, 1502, they reached a **bay**, which they named Rio de Janeiro. They sailed farther south, but historians are not sure how far they traveled. After facing bad weather, they sailed home and arrived in Lisbon on September 7, 1502.

Vespucci's third voyage was also with Coelho. On this trip Vespucci captained one of the six ships. They left Lisbon in May 1503. When they neared Brazil, Vespucci was sent ahead to explore. A second ship soon followed. They sailed as far south as southern Brazil and waited for the other ships. Finally they sailed back to Portugal without the others. The two ships arrived in Lisbon on June 28, 1504.

Telling the World

Had Amerigo Vespucci been Spanish or Portuguese, he would have written about what he had seen to the Spanish or Portuguese rulers. These letters probably would have been kept secret. Spain and Portugal did not want people in other countries to learn too much about their new land. Because Vespucci was from Florence, he reported what he had learned to the Florentine leaders instead.

In 1502, Vespucci wrote a letter about his 1501 voyage to his former **employer**, Lorenzo the Popolano. He described the land, its animals, and its people. When Vespucci returned from his third voyage in 1504, Lorenzo had died. Therefore, he wrote to the **prime minister** of Florence, Piero Soderini. Copies of the letters were passed around Florence, **translated** into Latin, and **published**. Later they were published in many other languages. In the letters Vespucci wrote of "what we may rightly call a New World . . . a **continent** more **densely** peopled and **abounding** in animals than our Europe or Asia or Africa."

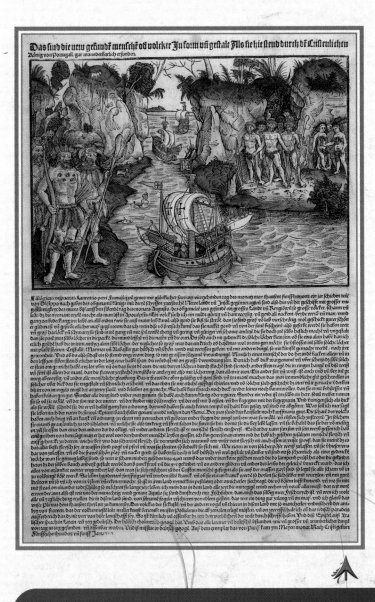

This is a page from "Mundus Novus," which is a letter about Vespucci's voyages to the New World. Vespucci had written to Lorenzo the Popolano, a member of the Medici family, around 1502. His letter became known as "Mundus Novus" after it was printed in Latin in 1504. This page from "Mundus Novus" was printed in German in 1505. Mundus novus is Latin for "new world."

When Vespucci wrote about his mysterious voyage of 1497, Spain and Portugal were not allowed to sail in each other's territory. Both countries sometimes did, though. These voyages were secret. Vespucci may have had some knowledge about these secret voyages that he wanted to share with his friends in Florence. Therefore, he may have pretended to have gained that information on an earlier voyage, such as his voyage of 1497.

From "Mundus Novus"

"The land of those areas is very fertile and pleasant, there are many hills and mountains, numerous valleys and grand rivers . . . Large trees grow there without cultivation and many of the trees bear fruit that is wonderful to eat and good for the human body . . ."

Vespucci wrote about the beauty of the New World.

This is Martin Waldseemüller's 1507 map of the world. This map was the first to use the name America for the new lands across the Atlantic Ocean. America is at the far left.

This is a detail, or a close-up, from Martin Waldseemüller's second map of the world, which was printed in 1513. Amerigo Vespucci is shown standing beside the lands in modern-day South America that Waldseemüller has called America.

The Naming of America

One of the people who read Amerigo Vespucci's letters was Martin Waldseemüller, a geography **professor** at a college in Saint-Dié, Lorraine, part of modern-day France. The professor was editing a book, *Cosmographiae Introductio*. In his book he printed Vespucci's letter to Piero Soderini, in which Vespucci claimed his first trip to the New World was in 1497. He also made the suggestion, "The fourth part of the globe, which since Americus discovered it, may be called Amerige or Land of Americus, or America." On a map Waldseemüller produced in 1507, he printed the word "America" on what is modern-day South America. The map was widely used, and other mapmakers began using the name for both North America and South America.

In 1505, Vespucci returned to Spain. Spain was one country where writers and mapmakers did not use the name America. They continued to call the New World *las Indias*, or "the Indies." Historians do not know if Vespucci realized that the New World had been named for him.

Death and Dishonor

Not long after his return to Spain, Amerigo Vespucci became a Spanish citizen. On March 22, 1508, he was named pilot major of Spain. As pilot major he decided which men were skilled enough to be pilots, the people who made sure that ships reached where they were going. The pilot major was also in charge of keeping the world maps used by Spanish ships up-to-date. Vespucci also ran a school for navigators, or the people who chose in what direction the ships should be sailed. Vespucci held these jobs until his death at age 57 on February 22, 1512. He was buried in the Vespucci family burial place in Florence.

When he died in 1512, Amerigo Vespucci was well respected. However, fewer than 100 years later, almost everyone thought he had tried to steal the glory for America's discovery from Christopher Columbus. However, by then it was too late. People liked the name America. They did not want to stop using it.

Timeline

1454 Amerigo Vespucci is born in Florence, Italy.

1492 Vespucci moves to Seville, Spain. Christopher Columbus is the first European to discover America.

1495 Vespucci's partner Gianetto Berardi dies, and Vespucci becomes the head of his business.

1497 Vespucci later says he went on his first voyage of exploration. Records show, though, that he was doing business in Spain.

1499 Vespucci sails with an expedition led by Alonso de Ojeda. They reach the mainland of South America.

1501 Vespucci sails with a Portuguese expedition led by Gonzalo Coelho. They explore the coast of Brazil and points farther south.

1502 Vespucci writes to Lorenzo the Popolano about his 1501 voyage.

1503 Vespucci sails with Coelho again and explores the coast of Brazil.

1504 Vespucci writes a letter to Piero Soderini about all his voyages, including the one made in 1497.

1507 On a map produced by Martin Waldseemüller, South America is labeled America, after Vespucci.

1512 Amerigo Vespucci dies and is buried in Florence, Italy.

AMERICVS VESPVCCI

Vespucci, shown in a 1500s painting, said that a book he had written about his New World voyages had been lent to a king. The king, however, never returned the book to Vespucci.

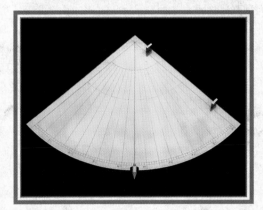

This is a quadrant, which explorers used in celestial navigation. They would find Polaris, the North Star, and line it up at the top of the quadrant. The curved edge had numbers that were used to judge a location in comparison to Polaris.

Understanding Vespucci

Those accusing, or charging, Amerigo Vespucci of dishonesty pointed out that Vespucci did not lead any of the expeditions on which he sailed. In his letters Vespucci never claimed to have led the expeditions. However, he never named the men who had.

When Vespucci wrote his letters, he did not know that they were going to be published. He was writing to people who knew him. These people probably already knew that Vespucci had not led the expeditions. Vespucci was writing to tell his friends what he had learned about the new land. He did it so successfully that the information traveled throughout Europe. Vespucci probably believed that America was close to Asia, just as Columbus had. Even if Vespucci was not the first to reach the mainland, he wrote about America as something completely new.

Vespucci's letters made people start thinking about America in a totally different way. That is why the great new land was named after him.

Glossary

abounding (eh-BOWND-ing) Having a large amount of something.

adviser (ed-VY-zur) A person who helps others make decisions.

assistant (uh-SIS-tunt) Someone who helps.

bay (BAY) A part of the ocean, close to land, where a ship can stay.

behaved (bih-HAYVD) Acted.

continent (KON-teh-nent) One of Earth's seven large landmasses. The continents are Europe, Asia, Africa, North America, South America, Antarctica, and Australia.

credit (KREH-dit) The honor that someone who does something special gets.

densely (DENTS-ly) Closely packed together or thick.

employer (im-PLOY-er) A person or a business that hires one or more people for wages.

expedition (ek-spuh-DIH-shun) A trip for a special purpose.

Garden of Eden (GAR-den UV EE-den) In the Bible, the garden where Adam and Eve, the first people, lived.

geography (jee-AH-gruh-fee) The study of Earth's weather, land, countries, people, and businesses.

investors (in-VES-turz) People who give money for something they hope will bring them more money later.

legal (LEE-gul) Allowed by the law.

mainland (MAYN-land) A large area of land near an island.

navigation (na-vuh-GAY-shun) The act of guiding a ship, an aircraft, or a rocket.

pope (POHP) The leader of the Roman Catholic Church.

prime minister (PRYM MIH-neh-ster) The leader of a government.

professor (preh-FEH-ser) A teacher at a college, or a school for advanced students.

published (PUH-blishd) Printed so that people can read it.

support (suh-PORT) Aid needed to fight for or against a cause.

trade route (TRAYD ROOT) The path used to travel places to buy or to sell goods.

translated (tranz-LAYT-ed) To have taken words from one language and turned them into another.

Treaty of Tordesillas (TREE-tee UV tawr-day-SEEL-yos) A 1494 agreement between Portugal and Spain that gave Portugal control over Brazil and Newfoundland.

voyage (VOY-ij) A journey by water.

Index

Web Sites

Due to the changing nature of Internet links, PowerKids Press has developed an online list of Web sites related to the subject of this book. This site is updated regularly. Please use this link to access the list:
www.powerkidslinks.com/pslfe/vespucci/

Primary Sources

Page 5. Left. Vespucci at Sea. (*detail*) Color engraving. 1596. From *Americae*, part IV. By Theodore de Bry. Kunstbibliothek, Staatliche Museen zu Berlin, Berlin, Germany. **Page 6. Left.** Lorenzo the Magnificent. Portrait. 1500s. Anonymous. Uffizi, Florence, Italy. **Page 10.** *Lettera delle isole nuouamente trouate in Quattro suoi viaggi.* (Italian for "the letter concerning the islands newly discovered on his four voyages"). By Amerigo Vespucci. Published by Bernard Quartich. 1885. This is a facsimile, or exact copy, of the letter published in Florence in the early 1500s. **Page 13. Bottom.** World Map. (*detail*) Circa 1544. By Battista Agnese. Library of Congress, Geography and Map Division, Washington, D.C. PowerKids Press added the heavy line for the Treaty of Tordesillas. **Page 14. Bottom.** Aztec. (*detail*) Pen Drawing. 1529. From the *Trachtenbuch* (German for *Costumebook*). By Christopher Weiditz. When Weiditz visited Spain in 1529, he made a group of drawings of the Aztecs who came to Spain with Cortes. **Page 17.** Page from the German edition of "Mundus Novus." Woodcut. 1505. Published in Leipzig. Herzog August Bibliothek, Wolfenbüttel, Germany. **Page 18. Top.** World Map. Woodblock print. 1507. By Martin Waldseemüller. Staatsbibliothek zu Berlin, Berlin, Germany. **Page 18. Bottom.** World Map. (*detail*). 1513. By Martin Waldseemüller. Staatsbibliothek zu Berlin, Berlin, Germany. **Page 21. Top.** Amerigo Vespucci. Portrait. 1500s. Probably a copy by Cristofano dell'Altissimo of an earlier portrait. Uffizi, Florence, Italy. **Page 21. Bottom.** Mariner's Quadrant. Brass. Circa 1600. National Maritime Museum, London, U.K.